D1514970

SPACE MISSIONS
OF THE 21ST CENTURY

BY ARNOLD RINGSTAD

Published by The Child's World®
1980 Lookout Drive • Mankato, MN 56003-1705
800-599-READ • www.childsworld.com

Acknowledgments
The Child's World®: Mary Berendes, Publishing Director
Red Line Editorial: Design, editorial direction, and production
Photographs ©: Space Science Institute/JPL/National Aeronautics and Space
Administration, cover, 1; Space Science Institute/JPL-Caltech/ National Aeronautics
and Space Administration, 4, 23; USGS/ASI/JPL-Caltech/ National Aeronautics and
Space Administration, 6; Walter Myers/Stocktrek Images/Corbis, 8; APL/SwRI/National
Aeronautics and Space Administration, 11; Rex Features/AP Images, 12; Red Line
Editorial/Shutterstock Images, 14; Demotix Live News/Demotix/Corbis, 16; National
Aeronautics and Space Administration, 18; Chris O'Meara/AP Images, 20

ISBN 9781634074797

LCCN 2015946219

Printed in the United States of America
Mankato, MN
December, 2015
PA02280

ABOUT THE AUTHOR

Arnold Ringstad is the author of more than 30 books for kids. He loves
reading and writing about space exploration. He lives in Minnesota.

TABLE OF
CONTENTS

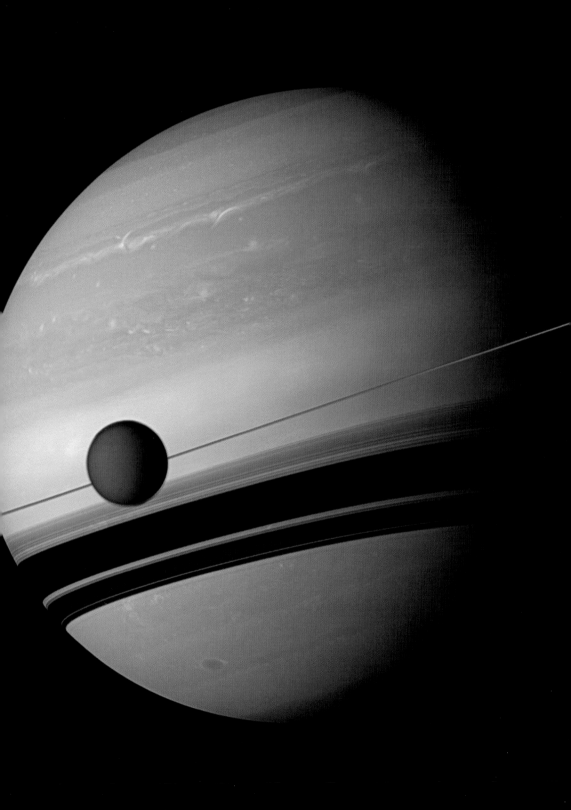

Chapter 1

MYSTERIES OF THE GAS GIANT

In late 1997, a huge Titan IV rocket shot into the Florida sky. At the top of the rocket was the *Cassini* spacecraft. Within a few minutes, *Cassini* was in space. It was headed for Saturn. This giant ringed planet is made up of swirling gases. Saturn is extremely far away. *Cassini* would take about seven years to reach it. When *Cassini* arrived, it would carry out one of the first major space missions of the 21st century.

Cassini is one of the largest spacecraft ever launched. It is about the size of a school bus. Scientists packed it with equipment for studying Saturn and its moons. *Cassini*'s cameras would take beautiful photographs. Sensors would measure Saturn's **gravity** and temperatures. Radar would map the surfaces of Saturn's moons.

◄ Titan, one of Saturn's many moons, orbits around the planet.

▲ **A colorized view of Titan's surface, with lakes in blue and rocks in yellow**

Previous spacecraft had flown past Saturn. But *Cassini* would be the first to go into **orbit** around the ringed planet. That meant it could study Saturn for several years. On July 1, 2004, *Cassini* flew between two of Saturn's rings as it approached the planet. It was time for the mission to begin.

Inside *Cassini* was a lander. This smaller ship was called *Huygens*. It would study Saturn's moon Titan. On Christmas Day 2004, springs on *Cassini* pushed the 700-pound (318-kg) lander toward Titan. *Huygens* moved through space at more than 13,000 miles per hour (20,900 km/h). Twenty-one days later, it arrived.

Titan's thick nitrogen **atmosphere** slowed *Huygens* down. The ship's parachute popped open. *Huygens* drifted slowly downward. As it fell, it took photos of its surroundings. The photos showed what looked like a long shoreline. But Titan does not have liquid water. Instead, it has large lakes made up of the chemicals ethane and methane.

Huygens hit the surface and bounced a little. The ship wobbled back and forth as it settled. It had landed safely on Titan. But *Huygens* could not move around. It could study only the area where it landed. Its equipment and sensors taught scientists a great deal about Titan. *Huygens* even sent back a photo from the surface. The picture showed pebbles, dust, and a hazy horizon.

Huygens was designed to last only a few hours. Its batteries ran out soon after landing on Titan. It still sits on the moon's surface today. And *Cassini* continues orbiting Saturn. Scientists believe it will keep sending information back to Earth for many years to come.

Cassini–Huygens is just one of many exciting space missions of the early 21st century. Other recent missions have taken spacecraft to the outer edge of our solar system. Some have landed on **comets**. Still others are paving the way for the first astronauts on Mars.

Chapter 2

EXPLORING PLUTO

The year was 1930. Astronomer Clyde Tombaugh spent days staring at stars. He worked at an **observatory** in Arizona. A powerful telescope there took pairs of photos days apart. Stars are so far away from Earth that they stay in the same spot in both photos. Anything that moves is much closer to Earth. It could even be a planet. Astronomers looked back and forth between pairs of photos. They wanted to find objects that moved. On February 18, Tombaugh spotted a tiny moving speck. He had discovered a **dwarf planet**. It was soon named Pluto.

Seventy-six years later, in 2006, a huge rocket blasted away from Earth. For the first time, a spacecraft was on its way to Pluto. Its name was *New Horizons*. The ship was much lighter than most other space probes. Why was it so small? The answer lies in the great distance from Earth to Pluto. Up to 4.67 billion miles (7.5 billion km) separate the two bodies. To travel so far, *New Horizons* had to move fast. And to move fast, the spacecraft

◀ **An artist's concept of *New Horizons* passing by Pluto** had to be light. The lighter an object is, the faster a rocket can push it.

New Horizons set a new speed record. It cruised through space at nearly 35,000 miles per hour (55,500 km/h). But New Horizons had no room for engines that could slow it down at Pluto. It would have to study Pluto as it zoomed past. The spacecraft would be close to Pluto for just a few months. Then it would leave the dwarf planet behind. It would fly farther into deep space. So, it had only one chance to complete the mission.

The spacecraft flew silently through space for nine years. In January 2015, it woke up. Scientists turned it on and tested its equipment. Had New Horizons survived the journey?

The mission team cheered when the ship responded to their signals. New Horizons was working. It aimed its cameras at Pluto. The dwarf planet was still millions of miles away. But the spacecraft got closer every day. Mission leader Alan Stern announced, "We've completed the longest journey any spacecraft has flown from Earth to reach its primary target, and we are ready to begin exploring."[1] In July 2015, New Horizons flew past Pluto. The spacecraft took detailed measurements and gathered lots of data. The mission was a huge success!

New Horizons discovered that Pluto has a heart-shaped region ▶ measuring 1,000 miles (1,600 km) across.

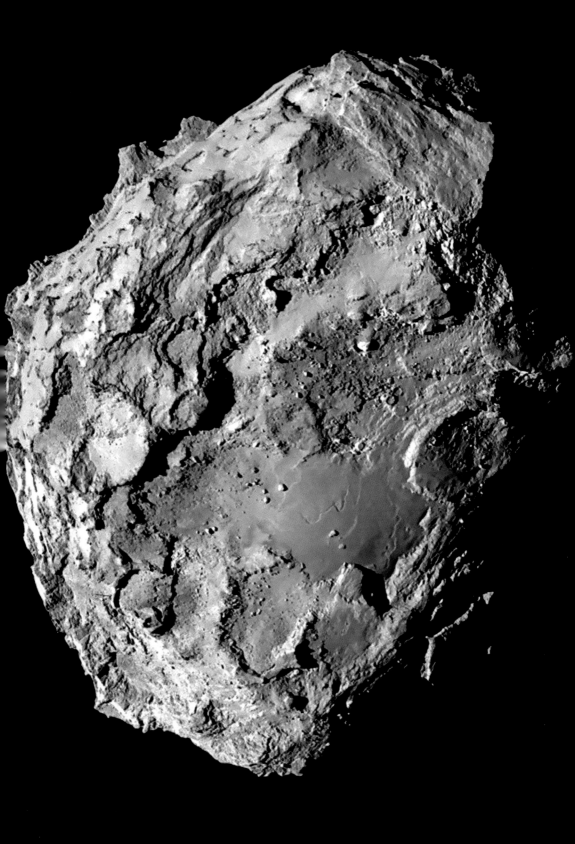

Chapter 3

LANDING ON A COMET

On March 2, 2004, an Ariane 5 rocket sat on its launch pad in French Guiana, South America. At the rocket's tip was an amazing new spacecraft called *Rosetta*. *Rosetta* would study a comet called 67P. The spacecraft would even drop a small lander called *Philae* onto the comet. This lander would study the comet's surface. The mission was the first ever to attempt a comet landing. But before *Rosetta* reached 67P, it had to escape Earth's gravity.

A crackling roar burst forth as the rocket's engine fired. The huge rocket, taller than a 15-story building, began lifting off the pad. Its flames lit up the night sky. The rocket pushed *Rosetta* up through Earth's atmosphere. Within a few minutes, the ship was in outer space.

Getting into space was easy compared to reaching 67P. *Rosetta* took a long, looping route through the solar system. By swinging past planets, it could use their gravity to boost its speed and

◀ **Comet 67P is less than 3 miles (5 km) wide.**

change its direction. *Rosetta* first flew past Earth in 2005. In 2007, it flew near Mars. Later that year, it flew past Earth again. Finally, it swung past Earth a third time in 2009. These moves put *Rosetta* on course to arrive at 67P in August 2014.

THE PATH OF *ROSETTA*

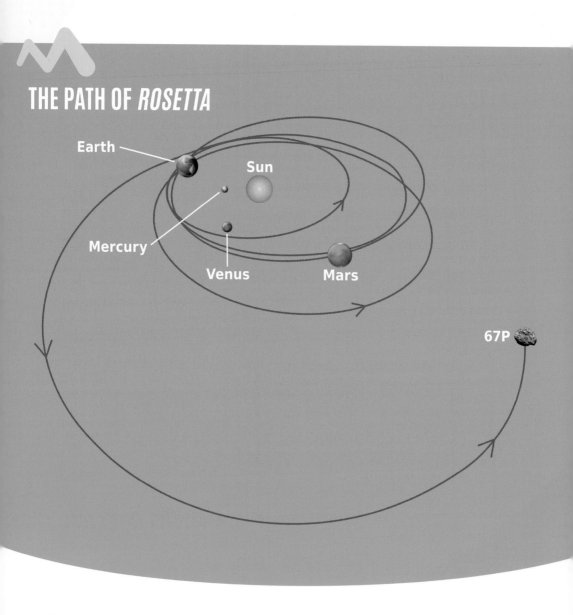

When *Rosetta* reached 67P, it took photos of the comet. It beamed the images back to Earth. Scientists studied them. They searched for a good landing site for *Philae*. When they found one, they commanded *Rosetta* to release *Philae*. The tiny lander was a box the size of a dishwasher. It had three metal legs. It drifted slowly down to the comet's surface.

67P is just a few miles wide. That means its gravity is much weaker than Earth's. If *Philae* landed too hard, it might bounce back into space. Luckily, **engineers** planned for this. *Philae* had hooks that would shoot downward. The hooks were designed to hold the lander to the comet. But as the spacecraft neared the ground, the hooks failed.

Philae hit the ground hard and bounced high. But the comet's gravity gently tugged the lander downward. Nearly two hours later, it bounced a second time. After a few smaller bounces, *Philae* finally came to rest. History's first comet landing had been successful.

However, the mission team soon realized there was a problem. *Philae* had settled in a shadow. The spacecraft relied on **solar panels** for power. The lander's batteries could power it for a few days. But it would need sunlight to keep working beyond that. The mission team worked quickly to collect as much data as they could.

Eventually, signals from the lander stopped. The battery did not have enough power. Even so, team manager Stephan Ulamec announced the mission was a success. He said, "Prior to falling silent, the lander was able to transmit all science data. . . . This machine performed magnificently under tough conditions, and we can be fully proud of the incredible scientific success *Philae* has delivered."[2] Meanwhile, *Rosetta* continued flying around the comet. It studied 67P and listened for any faint signals from *Philae* below.

Scientists studied the amazing pictures and data sent back by *Rosetta* and *Philae*. They learned more about comets. For example, they learned what comets are made of. Scientists believe these icy, dusty space objects date back billions of years. They hope comets can teach us about the history of the solar system.

◄ *Rosetta* **captured a photo of a cliff on the surface of 67P.**

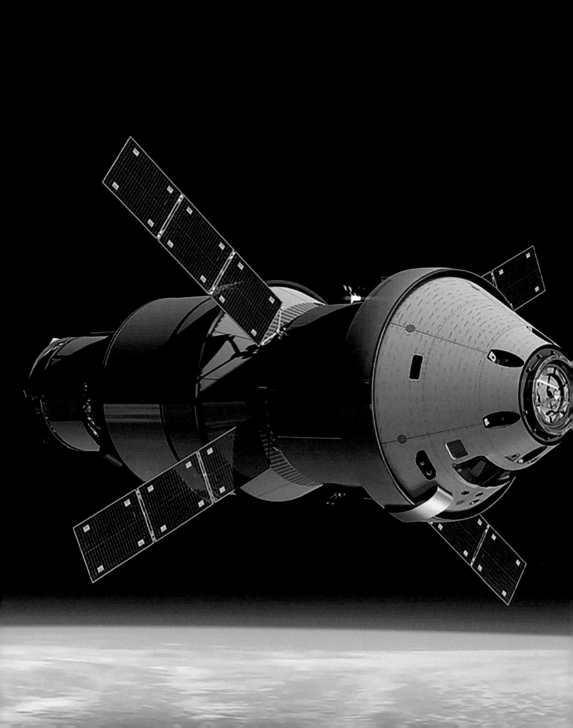

Chapter 4

THE ROAD TO MARS

Before people can set foot on Mars, they will need a spacecraft to take them there. Today's spacecraft cannot fly to Mars. But scientists and engineers are designing new ships that will. One of the most important is called Orion. It flew on its first test flight in December 2014.

Orion sat atop a Delta IV rocket on the Florida coast. The Orion spacecraft is shaped like a cone. On the outside, it looks similar to older spacecraft. But on the inside, it is packed with amazing technology. Glass touch screens replace the hundreds of switches used in the past. Advanced computers help the crew navigate in deep space. But for the December 2014 flight test, there were no people inside Orion. The spacecraft had to be tested to make sure it was safe. The mission was known as Exploration Flight Test 1, or EFT-1.

◀ **An artist's concept of the Orion spacecraft traveling above Earth**

▲ **The Orion spacecraft blasts off from Cape Canaveral on December 5, 2014.**

The mission controllers counted down the seconds until launch: "Eight, seven, six . . ."[3] Flames began shooting from the rocket's base. Its three enormous engines had started. They were building up to full power. The roar of the engines became louder and louder. The team continued the countdown: "Five, four, three, two, one."[4] The huge rocket began to lift off the pad. Flames poured out behind it as it climbed into the cloudy morning sky.

Orion soon reached space. It flew nearly 3,600 miles (5,800 km) from Earth. So far, the test was running perfectly. But Orion's biggest challenge was still ahead. It needed to return to Earth safely.

Earth's gravity began pulling Orion downward. The spacecraft's speed reached nearly 20,000 miles per hour (32,000 km/h). Such amazing speeds heated the air in front of the spacecraft. Orion's heat shield would protect it during the fiery reentry.

Orion plunged into Earth's atmosphere. Flames covered its heat shield. Chunks of the shield began burning away. Fortunately, they were designed to do this. Tiny pieces of the heat shield broke off. They carried dangerous heat away with them.

The spacecraft fell like a stone toward the Pacific Ocean. Suddenly, three orange-and-white parachutes emerged from the top of the capsule. They popped open into huge circles as the air caught them. Orion drifted down to a gentle landing among the waves. The scientists back at mission control cheered. EFT-1 had been a major success. It was one of the first important steps for a mission to Mars.

GLOSSARY

atmosphere (AT-muh-sfeer): An atmosphere is the layer of air that surrounds a planet. Rockets carry spacecraft out of Earth's atmosphere.

comets (KAHM-itz): Comets are a large chunks of ice and dust that orbit the sun. Some comets take thousands of years to orbit the sun.

dwarf planet (DWORF PLA-nit): A dwarf planet is an object in space that is smaller than a planet. Pluto is a dwarf planet.

engineers (en-juh-NEERZ): Engineers are people who design and build things. Spacecraft engineers create the ships that explore our solar system.

gravity (GRAV-uh-tee): Gravity is the force that pulls things together. Larger objects have stronger gravity, so the gravity of 67P is much weaker than Earth's.

observatory (uh-ZERV-uh-tohr-ee): An observatory is a place where astronomers study the sky using telescopes. Clyde Tombaugh discovered Pluto at an observatory in Arizona.

orbit (OR-bit): An orbit is the circular or oval-shaped path an object takes around a star or planet. The *Cassini* spacecraft is traveling in an orbit around Saturn.

solar panels (SOH-lur PAN-uhls): Solar panels are devices that turn the sun's light into electricity. The *Philae* lander used solar panels to power itself.

SOURCE NOTES

1. "NASA's New Horizons Spacecraft Begins First Stages of Pluto Encounter." *NASA*. NASA, 15 Jan. 2015. Web. 2 Jun. 2015.

2. "Our Lander's Asleep." *European Space Agency*. European Space Agency, 15 Nov. 2014. Web. 2 Jun. 2015.

3. "Launch of Orion EFT-1 on Delta IV Heavy, The First Step to Mars." *YouTube*. YouTube, 5 Dec. 2014. Web. 2. Jun. 2015.

4. Ibid.

TO LEARN MORE

Books

O'Brien, Patrick. *You Are the First Kid on Mars*. New York: G. P. Putnam's Sons, 2009.

Owens, L. L. *Pluto and Other Dwarf Planets*. Mankato, MN: Child's World, 2011.

Stott, Carole. *Space Exploration*. New York: DK, 2014.

Web Sites

Visit our Web site for links about space missions of the 21st century: childsworld.com/links

Note to Parents, Teachers, and Librarians: We routinely verify our Web links to make sure they are safe and active sites. So encourage your readers to check them out!

INDEX